The Suffering Servant's Courage

A Scriptural Rosary by Christine Haapala
Illustrations by Gustave Doré

Suffering Servant Scriptorium

Fairfax, Virginia

www.sufferingservant.com

Published with Ecclesiastical Permission
Diocese of Arlington
November 21, 2000

ISBN 0-9703996-5-0

Manufactured in the United States of America

Dedicated to
Our Lady of Perpetual Help

Special thanks to Father Michael Duesterhaus for his spiritual direction and encouragement.

Special appreciation to Father Matthew Carr for his inspirational sermon about people who practice the virtue of courage in their ministries of service.

In loving gratitude to my husband, Kenneth, and our three girls, Alison, Ellen and Mari.

Table of Illustrations

Table of Contents

Author's Note

In <u>The Secret of the Rosary</u>, St. Louis de Montfort warns us that reciting "the Rosary without meditating on the sacred mysteries would be a body without a soul." Pope Paul VI in *Marialis cultus (February 2, 1974)* stated that reciting the Rosary without contemplation is "mechanical repetition," thereby counseling us against the danger of praying a one-dimensional Rosary. Rosary praying requires both vocal prayer and thoughtful mental prayer. Meditation on the mysteries of the Rosary can be, at times, quite difficult, but praying a Scriptural Rosary simplifies, and spiritually edifies the meditation of the mysteries. By interweaving Sacred Scripture verses between the Rosary prayers of the *Our Father* and the *Hail Mary*, we enter into a dialogue with God in the presence of the Blessed Virgin Mary.

The inspiration for this book's meditation theme, courage, came during a sermon given by Father Matthew Carr (see his foreword *On the Importance of Being the Suffering Servant*). In his sermon, he spoke about how we are called to be active in our support of the needs of different ministries of the Catholic Church. One of the several ministries he mentioned was COURAGE.

When we join our works with prayer in concert with God's will, we are necessarily led to follow Him to the cross and join our sufferings with His. The Suffering Servant's Courage focuses on imitating the virtues of Jesus and Mary, in particular, fortitude and courage. We can draw strength from following their example.

Throughout Jesus and Mary's lives, they faced many hardships that required virtuous acts of courage. Mary silently suffered the humiliation of rejection and the threat of divorce when her pregnancy was discovered. While pregnant, Mary traveled across the arid, barren desert to help her, also pregnant, elderly cousin, Elizabeth. Joseph and Mary, poor and away from home, brought Jesus into the world in the humble surroundings of a cold, dingy stable.

Prior to his Passion, Jesus prayed in the Garden of Gethsemane, but three of his apostles could not even spend one hour with him, instead, they slept. Later that evening, two of his closest apostles betrayed him. Judas sold him for thirty pieces of silver and St. Peter denied him three times. Only one of Jesus' apostles, St. John, followed him to the cross. Mary carried Simeon's prophecy in her heart for thirty-three years and stood at the foot of the cross to watch her Son's heart pierced by a lance. Then, she lost her first-born to the heinous death of crucifixion. Mary witnessed the Christian persecutions during the early years of the Catholic Church.

As we pray, let us ask that God continue to bless us and provide us strength and courage sufficient for the day and may the Blessed Virgin Mary be with us now and at the hour of death. We have the strength to ask this special favor of her, because she had the courage to be at the hour of Jesus' death.

Fairfax, Virginia
October, 2000

Author's Note to the Second Edition

Praying the Most Holy Rosary is so very easy and yet, many are fooled by its simplicity and power, thus avoid it. We can only caution against this delusion by echoing St Louis de Montfort's warning that "To think it is possible to say prayers that are finer and more beautiful than the Our Father and the Hail Mary is to fall prey to a strange illusion of the devil. / These heavenly prayers are the support, strength, and safeguard of our souls." (*25th Rose, The Secret of the Rosary*) Similarly, St. Thomas Aquinas calls the *Our Father*, the *Hail Mary* and the *Apostles' Creed* the three greatest prayers. In the Apostolic Letter on the Rosary of the Blessed Virgin Mary (*Rosarium Virginis Mariae, Oct 16th, 2002*), Pope John Paul II said the Most Holy Rosary is "a prayer so easy and yet so rich [that it] deserves to be rediscovered . . . Rediscover the Rosary in the light of Scripture . . ." A Scriptural Rosary richly enhances the meditation of the mysteries through Sacred Scriptures.

In this Apostolic letter, Pope John Paul II also recommended adding five additional mysteries – called the Luminous Mysteries – "to bring out fully the Christological depth of the Rosary . . ." This edition of <u>The Suffering Servant's Courage</u> has been updated to include these Luminous Mysteries with 18 additional pages. Also included are seven more pictures from Gustave Doré's Bible illustrations. The original fifteen mysteries remain as they appeared in the First Edition.

The theme of courage, fortitude and perseverance is revealed, as in the other mysteries, in these mysteries of light. Following his Baptism, Jesus was led to a high mountain to face temptations by the devil. These meditations contrast the weakness of Adam and Eve with the strength and courage of Christ under the same temptations. The wedding at Cana highlights Jesus' courage to begin his three-year ministry that culminates in accepting God's will – the perfect sacrifice – His death on the cross. Mary was there at the beginning of his ministry. Mary would be there during Jesus' final words on the Cross. By witnessing Jesus' Transfiguration, the apostles have a beacon to guide them. Soon, Jesus would not be with them, so the apostles by focusing on this glimpse of the beauty and glory of eternity can find the strength and courage for the tough times ahead.

We pray that through the intercession and the prayers of the Blessed Virgin Mary, she will bring us and the whole world closer to her Divine Son, Jesus Christ – the King of Mercy.

Fairfax, Virginia
February, 2003

Foreword

On the Importance of Being
the Suffering Servant

The Suffering Servant is a figure described in the Book of the Prophet Isaiah. Indeed, its direct and indirect use by Our Lord Jesus Christ and its vast role in the life of the Church had led the Fathers to refer to this book as the "Fifth Gospel." Whether directly or by allusion, the Book of the Prophet Isaiah stands behind much of the New Testament. Moreover, it is particularly the image of the Suffering Servant, as described by the Four Songs of the Suffering Servant of the Lord, *(Is 42:1-4; 49:1-7; 50:4-11; 52:13-15; 53)* that Jesus takes and combines with the Son of Man prophecy from Daniel 7 to explain the kind of Messiah He is.

We see throughout the Gospels that Our Lord is reluctant to reveal Himself as the Messiah because of his credible fear that the crowd would want him to become their king. But their messianic expectations for a new King David or King Solomon, who would restore Israel to her proper place, full of power, glory and wealth, was not his mission. Rather, Christ came to proclaim a kingdom not of this world whose marks were not power, glory and wealth, but justice, peace and joy. The Suffering Servant stands in marked contrast to the human expectations of Jesus' contemporaries, whether they be his disciples or his enemies. Jesus connects his mission with the Suffering Servant by conforming Himself to what is described in the Fourth Song.

> *Yet it was our infirmities that he bore, our sufferings*
> *   that he endured...*
> *Upon him was the chastisement that makes us whole,*
> *by his stripes we were healed...*
> *he surrendered himself to death*
> *and was counted among the wicked;*
> *And he shall take away the sins of many,*
> *and win pardon for their offenses.*
> *Is 53:4-5,12*

Isaiah 53 sounds like an eyewitness account of Jesus' passion, but it was written hundreds of years before He was born.

At the Last Supper He established the Eucharist whereby his disciples would understand the meaning of his entire life. During the Mass when the priest takes the cup filled with wine, we hear him echo the words of Jesus.

> *"This cup is the new covenant in my blood. Do this,*
> *whenever you drink it, in remembrance of me." Every*
> *time, then, you eat this bread and drink this cup, you*
> *proclaim the death of the Lord until he comes!*
> *1Cor 11:25-26*

Christ did not need to say that He was the Suffering Servant because what He did and said made that clear. He was the Servant who was prophesied to come who would bear the sins of others for their redemption. Christ Crucified has spoken to us his final and complete word about the meaning of love and the mystery of God. Jesus - love incarnate - did what love does: suffers for others and pours out his entire life - sacrifices all - for the good of another, indeed for the good of every other.

But what of us? Jesus had definite notions about how we should follow his example of other-centered love. He spent his entire public ministry proclaiming this fact by word and deed. And just in case the apostles missed it - and they did - he told them again emphatically at the Last Supper - where he washed their feet and instituted the Holy Eucharist - when he said to them "I give you a new commandment: love one another as I have loved you."

Jesus recognized that the word love - then as now - had lost its power and meaning and had been reduced to describe less profound realities than the one to which his entire life witnessed. He gave them the definition of love on the Cross and prepared them for this definition by his teaching and life.

He told them earlier at the Mount of Beatitude, that if they love those who love them, what merit is there in that: pagans and sinners do as much! He told them that they should love their neighbor and even their enemy. Little did they understand what Jesus meant. Later, St. Paul explains this unbelievable truth in Romans 5:8 when he wrote "But God shows his love for us in that while we were yet sinners, Christ died for us." As Jesus taught them about love for their neighbors, their enemies, the Apostles did not realize he was speaking of his love for them and for us.

So the love into which we have been baptized and which we are called to live every day to every person is none other than that same love of Christ. This is impossible for us to do. We can never love as Christ, except if we realize that it is He who will give us what we need to do what is impossible. So our loving as he loves is possible because he has chosen to give us this power - the Holy Spirit.

When the Holy Spirit comes into our hearts through the grace of the sacraments, our prayers and sacrifices and our works of mercy, we are given the strength to do what is impossible: to love as he has loved us. This strength, deriving from the Passion of Our Lord Jesus Christ, must necessarily include the gift and fruit of the Holy Spirit: courage. Courage is that cardinal virtue whose principal act is the will to fall in battle in defense of the Truth and that gift by which you and I have the strength, perseverance, patience and endurance to go where Jesus wishes us to go: into places of darkness (for we are the light of the world) and places of violence (for we are peace-makers and thus children of God).

With courage we can recognize this world is a spiritual battle-ground between the Kingdom of God that Jesus began and to which his martyrs throughout the centuries have witnessed and the counter-Kingdom of the world. With eyes wide open to this truth and sealed with the gift that is the Holy Spirit - as was said when we were confirmed - we take up our places along the frontlines between the Kingdom of justice, peace and joy and the counter-Kingdom of injustice, violence and bitterness. Armed with love, truth and courage we go in our daily lives to confront a world still in need of the power of the Gospel - a world that we discover within the unredeemed parts of our heart, habits and opinions and those of our society.

To love as the Suffering Servant means to follow the path of self-sacrifice - a way that would be impossible without the courage of the Suffering Servant.

Father Matthew Carr
Holy Spirit Catholic Church
Annandale, Virginia
Feast of All Saints
A.D. 2000

Introduction

Over the years I have heard many Catholics say that they found the Rosary monotonous, particularly at wakes. One young priest told the deceased's daughters that we are not going to say the Rosary; instead we will read Holy Scripture. Christine Haapala's Scriptural Rosary, with illustrations by Gustave Doré, is anything but boring. It helps one to pray the Rosary, while **really** meditating on each of the fifteen mysteries in the lives of Jesus and Mary. Of course, it will take a little more time, but time well spent with Jesus and Mary. The Scriptural texts are most apt, and the art of Doré enables one to contemplate the life of the Suffering Servant who redeemed us by His suffering, death, and Resurrection. I suggest that it be given to grade school children in the presence of their parents. Everyone can benefit by learning how to meditate upon these mysteries of Faith. Our Blessed Mother will be pleased.

October 3, 2000

Father John F. Harvey, OSFS
Director of COURAGE
New York City

The Suffering Servant's Courage

A Scriptural Rosary

The Joyful Mysteries

The Sign of the Cross

The Apostles' Creed

Rejoice to the extent that you share in the sufferings of Christ, so that when his glory is revealed you may also rejoice exultantly. *1Pt 4:13*

Our Father...

Consider it all joy, my brothers, when you encounter various trials, for you know that the testing of your faith produces perseverance. *Jas 1:2-3*

Hail Mary...

Be strong and take heart, / all you who hope in the LORD. *Ps 31:25*

Hail Mary...

'You shall love the Lord your God with all your heart, with all your soul, with all your mind, and with all your strength.' *Mk 12:30*

Hail Mary... Glory be... O My Jesus...

The First Joyful Mystery
The Annunciation

Joseph ... decided to divorce her quietly ... Wait for the LORD, take courage; / be stouthearted, wait for the LORD! *Mt 1:19, Ps 27:14*

Our Father...

Thus said the Lord GOD, / the Holy One of Israel: / By waiting and by calm you shall be saved, / in quiet and in trust your strength lies. *Is 30:15*

Hail Mary...

You need endurance to do the will of God and receive what he has promised. / "For, after just a brief moment, / he who is to come shall come; / he shall not delay." *Heb 10:36-37*

Hail Mary...

Bless the LORD, all you angels, / mighty in strength and attentive, obedient to every command. / ... Bless the LORD, my soul! *Ps 103:20,22*

Hail Mary...

The angel Gabriel was sent from God to a town of Galilee called Nazareth, to a virgin ... The angel said to her, "Do not be afraid, Mary, for you have found favor with God." *Lk 1:26-27,30*

Hail Mary...

THE ANNUNCIATION

I love you, LORD, my strength, / LORD, my rock, my fortress, my deliverer, / My God, my rock of refuge, / my shield, my saving horn, my stronghold! *Ps 18:2-3*

Hail Mary...

Fear not, I am with you; / be not dismayed; I am your God. / I will strengthen you, and help you. *Is 41:10*

Hail Mary...

Joseph ... unwilling to expose her to shame, decided to divorce her quietly ... Behold, the angel of the Lord appeared to him in a dream and said, "Joseph, son of David, do not be afraid to take Mary your wife into your home." *Mt 1:19-20*

Hail Mary...

There is no fear in love, but perfect love drives out fear... *1Jn 4:18*

Hail Mary...

Submit yourselves to God. ... Draw near to God, and he will draw near to you. ... Humble yourselves before the Lord and he will exalt you. *Jas 4:7-9*

Hail Mary...

My strength and my courage is the LORD, / and he has been my savior. ... Mary said: / ... "The Mighty One has done great things for me, / and holy is his name." *Ex 15:2, Lk 1:46,49*

Hail Mary... Glory be... O My Jesus...

The Second Joyful Mystery
The Visitation

Mary set out and traveled to the hill country in haste. ... Even when I walk through a dark valley, / I fear no harm for you are at my side; / your rod and staff give me courage. *Lk 1:39, Ps 23:4*

Our Father...

Happy are those who find refuge in you, / whose hearts are set on pilgrim roads. / ... They pass through outer and inner wall / and see the God of gods on Zion. *Ps 84:6,8*

Hail Mary...

O God, you are my God - / for you I long! / For you my body yearns; / for you my soul thirsts, / Like a land parched, lifeless, / and without water. *Ps 63:2*

Hail Mary...

I stretch out my hands to you; / I thirst for you like a parched land. / ... Show me the path I should walk, / for to you I entrust my life. *Ps 143:6,8*

Hail Mary...

During those days Mary set out and traveled to the hill country in haste to a town of Judah ... I will strengthen them in the LORD, / and they shall walk in his name, says the LORD. *Lk 1:39-40, Zec 10:12*

Hail Mary...

"The LORD has redeemed his servant / ... They did not thirst / when he led them through dry lands; / Water from the rock he set flowing for them; / he cleft the rock, and waters welled forth." *Is 48:20-22*

Hail Mary...

God, my Lord, is my strength; / he makes my feet swift as those of hinds / and enables me to go upon the heights ... "Do not fear ... the LORD, your God, is with you wherever you go." *Hb 3:19, Jos 1:9*

Hail Mary...

"Whoever drinks the water I shall give will never thirst; the water I shall give will become in him a spring of water welling up to eternal life." *Jn 4:14*

Hail Mary...

The burning sands will become pools, / and the thirsty ground, springs of water ... Those whom the LORD has ransomed will return / and enter Zion singing, / crowned with everlasting joy. *Is 35:7,10*

Hail Mary...

Blessed are they who hunger and thirst for righteousness, / for they will be satisfied. *Mt 5:6*

Hail Mary...

Mary said: / ... "My spirit rejoices in God my savior. / ... Behold, from now on will all ages call me blessed." *Lk 1:46-48*

Hail Mary... Glory be... O My Jesus...

7

The Third Joyful Mystery
The Nativity

There was no room for them in the inn … Blessed be the God and Father of our Lord Jesus Christ, the Father of compassion and God of all encouragement, who encourages us in our affliction. *Lk 2:7, 2Cor 1:3-4*

Our Father...

For over all, his glory will be shelter and protection: / shade from the parching heat of day, / refuge and cover from storm and rain. *Is 4:6*

Hail Mary...

For you know the gracious act of our Lord Jesus Christ, that for your sake he became poor although he was rich, so that by his poverty you might become rich. *2Cor 8:9*

Hail Mary...

[Mary] gave birth to her firstborn son … and laid him in a manger, because there was no room for them in the inn. *Lk 2:7*

Hail Mary...

May all who seek you / rejoice and be glad in you. / … Though I am afflicted and poor, / the Lord keeps me in mind. *Ps 40:17-18*

Hail Mary...

The shepherds said to one another, "Let us go, then, to Bethlehem to see this thing that has taken place, which the Lord has made known to us." *Lk 2:15*

Hail Mary...

THE NATIVITY

In your mercy you led the people you redeemed; / in your strength you guided them to your holy dwelling. *Ex 15:13*

Hail Mary...

Did not God choose those who are poor in the world to be rich in faith and heirs of the kingdom that he promised to those who love him? *Jas 2:5*

Hail Mary...

Rich and poor have a common bond: / the LORD is the maker of them all. *Prv 22:2*

Hail Mary...

[The Magi] were overjoyed at seeing the star, and on entering the house they saw the child with Mary his mother. ... They opened their treasures and offered him gifts of gold, frankincense, and myrrh. *Mt 2:10-11*

Hail Mary...

"Blessed are the poor in spirit, / for theirs is the kingdom of heaven." ... My strength and my courage is the LORD, / and he has been my savior. *Mt 5:3; Is 12:2*

Hail Mary... Glory be... O My Jésus...

THE WISE MEN GUIDED BY THE STAR

The Fourth Joyful Mystery
The Presentation of Jesus in the Temple

"You yourself a sword will pierce" ... Affliction produces endurance, and endurance, proven character ... the love of God has been poured out into our hearts through the holy Spirit. *Lk 2:35, Rom 5:3-5*

Our Father...

"Throughout the ages, every male among you, when he is eight days old, shall be circumcised." *Gn 17:12*

Hail Mary...

They took [Jesus] up to Jerusalem to present him to the Lord ... Simeon blessed them and said to Mary his mother, ... "you yourself a sword will pierce." *Lk 2:22,34-35*

Hail Mary...

He pierces my side without mercy, / ... He pierces me with thrust upon thrust. *Job 16:13-14*

Hail Mary...

LORD, do not stay far off; / my strength, come quickly to help me. / Deliver me from the sword. ... His mother kept all these things in her heart. *Ps 22:20-21, Lk 2:51*

Hail Mary...

I have great sorrow and constant anguish in my heart. *Rom 9:2*

Hail Mary...

"Do not let your hearts be troubled. You have faith in God."
Jn 14:1

Hail Mary...

They shall look on him whom they have thrust through, and they shall mourn for him as one mourns for an only son ... One soldier thrust his lance into his side. *Zec 12:10, Jn 19:34*

Hail Mary...

"You also are now in anguish. But I will see you again, and your hearts will rejoice, and no one will take your joy away from you."
Jn 16:22

Hail Mary...

I will praise you with all my heart, / glorify your name forever, Lord my God. ... You have rescued me from the depth.
Ps 86:12-13

Hail Mary...

Magnify the LORD with me; / let us exalt his name together. / I sought the LORD, who answered me, / delivered me from all my fears. *Ps 34:4-5*

Hail Mary... Glory be... O My Jesus...

The Fifth Joyful Mystery
The Finding of Jesus in the Temple

The boy Jesus remained behind in Jerusalem ... [Joseph and Mary] returned to Jerusalem to look for him. ... Encourage those who are in any affliction with the encouragement with which we ourselves are encouraged by God. *Lk 2:43,45, 2Cor 1:4*

Our Father...

When you call me, when you go to pray to me, I will listen to you. When you look for me, you will find me. Yes, when you seek me with all your heart. *Jer 29:12-13*

Hail Mary...

Those who seek the LORD understand all. ... After three days they found him in the temple, sitting in the midst of the teachers, listening to them and asking them questions. *Prv 28:5, Lk 2:46*

Hail Mary...

Thus says the Lord GOD: I swear I am coming against these shepherds. I will claim my sheep from them and put a stop to their shepherding my sheep so that they may no longer pasture themselves. I will save my sheep. *Ez 34:10*

Hail Mary...

For the Son of Man has come to seek and to save what was lost ... You, my sheep, you are the sheep of my pasture, and I am your God, says the Lord GOD. *Lk 19:10, Ez 34:31*

Hail Mary...

JESUS WITH THE DOCTORS

I myself will pasture my sheep; I myself will give them rest, says the Lord GOD. The lost I will seek out, the strayed I will bring back. *Ez 34:15-16*

Hail Mary...

The LORD is my shepherd ... Shepherd of Israel / ... From your throne upon the cherubim reveal yourself ... Like a shepherd he feeds his flock; / in his arms he gathers the lambs, / Carrying them in his bosom. *Ps 23:1, Ps 80:2, Is 40:11*

Hail Mary...

Lost sheep were my people, / their shepherds misled them, / straggling on the mountains; / From mountain to hill they wandered, / losing the way to their fold. *Jer 50:6*

Hail Mary...

If a man has a hundred sheep and one of them goes astray, will he not leave the ninety-nine in the hills and go in search of the stray ... In just the same way, it is not the will of your heavenly Father that one of these little ones be lost. *Mt 18:12,14*

Hail Mary...

"'Rejoice with me because I have found my lost sheep' ... There will be more joy in heaven over one sinner who repents." *Lk 15:6-7*

Hail Mary...

I became the shepherd of the flock to be slaughtered ... I am the good shepherd. A good shepherd lays down his life for the sheep. *Zec 11:7, Jn 10:11*

Hail Mary... Glory be... O My Jesus... Hail Holy Queen...

CHRIST IN THE SYNAGOGUE

JOHN THE BAPTIST PREACHING IN THE WILDERNESS

The Luminous Mysteries

The Sign of the Cross

The Apostles' Creed

[T]hrough the mercy shown us, we are not discouraged. ... [God] has shown in our hearts to bring to light the knowledge of the glory of God in the face of [Jesus] Christ. *2Cor 4:1,6*

Our Father...

A man named John was sent from God. He came for testimony, to testify to the light, so that all might believe through him. *Jn 1:6-7*

Hail Mary...

May our Lord Jesus Christ himself and God our Father, who has loved us and given us everlasting encouragement and good hope through his grace, encourage your hearts and strengthen them in every good deed and word. *2Thes 2:16-17*

Hail Mary...

I am your servant ... Truly I love your commands ... The revelation of your words sheds light, / gives understanding ... *Ps 119:125,127,130*

Hail Mary... Glory Be... O My Jesus...

The First Luminous Mystery
The Baptism of Jesus

After Jesus was baptized... a voice came from the heavens, saying, "This is my beloved Son, with whom I am pleased." Then Jesus was led by the Spirit into the desert to be tempted by the devil. *Mt 3:16-17, Mt 4:1*

Our Father...

When God, in the beginning, created man, / he made him subject to his own free choice. ... Now the serpent was the most cunning of all the animals that the LORD God had made. The serpent asked the woman, "Did God tell you not to eat from any of the trees in the garden?" *Sir 15:14, Gn 3:1*

Hail Mary...

I said to myself, "Come, now, let me try you with pleasure and the enjoyment of good things." But behold, this too was vanity. ... So humble yourselves under the mighty hand of God. ... Your opponent the devil is prowling around like a roaring lion looking for [someone] to devour. Resist him... *Ecc 2:1, 1Pt 5:6,8*

Hail Mary...

This is how you are to pray: / "Our Father in heaven ... deliver us from the evil one." ... The tempter approached and said to [Jesus], "If you are the Son of God, command that these stones become loaves of bread." *Mt 6:9,13, Mt 4:3*

Hail Mary...

But the serpent said to the woman: "You certainly will not die! No, God knows well that the moment you eat of it your eyes will be opened." ... [S]in is a demon lurking at the door: his urge is toward you, yet you can be his master." *Gn 3:4-5, Gn 4:7*

Hail Mary...

THE BAPTISM OF JESUS

THE TEMPTATION OF JESUS

[P]repare yourself for trials. ... [Jesus] remained in the desert for forty days. ... My knees totter from fasting; / my flesh has wasted away. ... Then the devil... made him stand on the parapet of the temple, and said to him, "If you are the Son of God, throw yourself down." *Sir 2:1, Mk 1:13, Ps 109:24, Mt 4:5-6*

Hail Mary...

[T]he serpent said to the woman: "... [Y]ou will be like gods who know what is good and what is bad." ... And the LORD said to Satan, "Whence do you come?" and Satan answered the LORD and said, "From roaming the earth ..." *Gn 3:4-5, Job 2:2*

Hail Mary...

Let Job be tried to the limit ... Blessed is the man who perseveres in temptation for when he has been proved he will receive the crown of life ... Thus the LORD blessed the latter days of Job more than his earlier ones. *Job 34:36, Jas 1:12, Job 42:12*

Hail Mary...

Then the devil took [Jesus] up to a very high mountain, and showed him all the kingdoms of the world in their magnificence, and he said to him, "All these I shall give to you, if you prostrate yourself and worship me." *Mt 4:8-9*

Hail Mary...

"Get away, Satan! It is written: / 'The Lord, your God shall you worship / and him alone shall you serve.'" ... When the devil had finished every temptation, he departed from him for a time. *Mt 4:10, Lk 4:13*

Hail Mary...

For we do not have a high priest who is unable to sympathize with our weaknesses, but one who has similarly been tested in every way, yet without sin. *Heb 4:15*

Hail Mary... Glory Be... O My Jesus...

The Second Luminous Mystery
The Wedding at Cana

Unless your faith is firm / you shall not be firm! / ... Therefore the Lord himself will give you this sign: the virgin shall be with child and bear a son. ... Blessed are you who believed that was spoken to you by the Lord would be fulfilled. *Is 7:9,14, Lk 1:45*

Our Father...

On the third day there was a wedding in Cana in Galilee, and the mother of Jesus was there. ... His mother said to the servers, "Do whatever he tells you." *Jn 2:1,5*

Hail Mary...

"[Y]ou have kept the good wine until now." Jesus did this as the beginning of his signs in Cana in Galilee and so revealed his glory, and his disciples began to believe in him. *Jn 2:10-11*

Hail Mary...

The works that the Father gave me to accomplish, these works that I perform testify on my behalf that the Father has sent me." *Jn 5:36*

Hail Mary...

[T]he blind men approached him and Jesus said to them, "Do you believe that I can do this?" "Yes, Lord," they said to him. Then he touched their eyes and said, "Let it be done for you according to your faith." And their eyes were opened. *Mt 9:28-30*

Hail Mary...

THE MARRIAGE IN CANA

Jesus said to him, "'If you can!' Everything is possible to one who has faith." Then the boy's father cried out, "I do believe, help my unbelief!" *Mk 9:23-24*

Hail Mary...

The Pharisees and Sadducees came and, to test him, asked him to show them a sign from heaven. ... "An evil and unfaithful generation seeks a sign, but no sign will be given it except the sign of Jonah." *Mt 16:1,4*

Hail Mary...

"What are we going to do? This man is performing many signs. If we leave him alone, all will believe in him." ... Although he had performed so many signs in their presence they did not believe in him. ... / "Lord, who has believed our preaching, / to whom has the might of the Lord been revealed?" *Jn 11:47-48, Jn 12:37-38*

Hail Mary...

Believe in the Lord Jesus and you and your household will be saved. ... "I am the resurrection and the life ... Do you believe this?" [Martha] said to him, "Yes, Lord. I have come to believe you are the Messiah." *Acts 16:31, Jn 11:25-27*

Hail Mary...

[Thomas] said to him, "My Lord and my God!" Jesus said to him, "Have you come to believe because you have seen me? Blessed are those who have not seen and have believed." *Jn 20:28-29*

Hail Mary...

"Believe me that I am in the Father and the Father is in me, or else, believe because of the works themselves." *Jn 14:11*

Hail Mary... Glory Be... O My Jesus...

The Third Luminous Mystery
Jesus' Ministry and Call to Conversion

Do not abandon me to the will of my foes; / malicious and lying witnesses have risen against me. / ... Wait for the LORD, take courage. *Ps 27:12,14*

Our Father...

Those who seek my life lay snares for me; / they seek my misfortune, they speak of ruin; / they plot treachery all the day. ... [T]hey plotted to kill him. They said to one another: "Here comes that master dreamer! Come on, let us kill him..." *Ps 38:13, Gen 37:18-20*

Hail Mary...

"[N]o prophet is accepted in his own native place." ... When the people in the synagogue heard this, they were all filled with fury. They rose up, drove him ... to the brow of the hill ... to hurl him down. ... I groan / at the uproar of the enemy, / the clamor of the wicked. *Lk 4:24,28-29, Ps 55:3-4*

Hail Mary...

The evil man lies in wait for blood, / and plots against your choicest possessions. ... [T]he chief priests and elders of the people assembled in the palace of the high priest ... and they consulted together to arrest Jesus. *Sir 11:32, Mt 26:3-4*

Hail Mary...

The scribes and the Pharisees watched him closely to see if he would cure on the sabbath so that they might discover a reason to accuse him. ... But they became enraged and discussed together what they might do to Jesus. ... They speak against me with lying tongues. ... In return for my love they slander me. *Lk 6:7,11, Ps 109:2,4*

Hail Mary...

JESUS HEALING THE SICK

[Jesus] said, "Woe also to you scholars of the law! You impose on people burdens hard to carry, but you yourselves do not lift one finger to touch them." ... [T]he scribes and Pharisees began to act with hostility toward him. *Lk 11:46,53*

Hail Mary...

"Beware of the leaven of the Pharisees and Sadducees." Then they understood that he was not telling them to beware of the leaven of bread, but of the teaching of the Pharisees and Sadducees." *Mt 16:11-12*

Hail Mary...

[P]reserve me from the violent, / who plot to trip me up. / The arrogant have set a trap for me; / villains have spread a net, / laid snares for me by the wayside. *Ps 140:5-6*

Hail Mary...

"[T]he Son of Man will be handed over to the chief priests and the scribes, and they will condemn him to death and hand him over to the Gentiles who will mock him, spit upon him, scourge him, and put him to death..." *Mk 10:33-34*

Hail Mary...

My ravenous enemies press upon me; / they close their hearts, / they fill their mouths with proud roaring. / Their steps even now encircle me. ... Satan entered into Judas, ... and he went to the chief priests and temple guards. *Ps 17:9-11, Lk 22:3-4*

Hail Mary...

[T]he Devil has come down to you in great fury, / for he knows he has but a short time." ... a trial of fire is occurring ... [T]hose who suffer in accord with God's will hand their souls over to a faithful creator. *Rv 12:12, 1Pt 4:12,19*

Hail Mary... Glory Be... O My Jesus...

The Fourth Luminous Mystery
The Transfiguration

During the fourth watch of the night, he came toward them, walking on the sea. ... "Take courage, it is I; do not be afraid." ... "I am ... the bright morning star." ... O Most High, when I am afraid, / in you I place my trust. *Mt 14:25,27, Rv 22:16, Ps 56:3-4*

Our Father...

Jesus took Peter, James, and John his brother, and led them up a high mountain by themselves. And he was transfigured before them; his face shone like the sun and his clothes became white as light. ... [W]hoever lives the truth comes to the light, so that his works may be clearly seen as done in God. *Mt 17:1-2, Jn 3:21*

Hail Mary...

Moses came down from Mount Sinai with the two tablets ... the skin of Moses' face was radiant ... Blessed is he who shall have seen you before he dies, / O Elijah. ... Peter said ... "If you wish, I will make three tents here, one for you, one for Moses, and one for Elijah." *Ex 34:29,35, Sir 48:11-12, Mt 17:4*

Hail Mary...

[A] bright cloud cast a shadow over them, then from the cloud came a voice that said, "This is my beloved Son, with whom I am well pleased; listen to him." *Mt 17:5*

Hail Mary...

[The disciples] fell prostrate and were very much afraid. But Jesus came and touched them, saying, "Rise, and do not be afraid." *Mt 17:6-7*

Hail Mary...

THE TRANSFIGURATION

[Y]ou furnished the flaming pillar / which was a guide on the unknown way. ... "Master, we do not know where you are going; how can we know the way." Jesus said to him, "I am the way and the truth and the life." *Wis 18:3, Jn 14:5-6*

Hail Mary...

I am the first and I am the last; / there is no God but me. ... Fear not, be not troubled: / did I not announce and foretell it long ago? ... From that time on, Jesus began to show his disciples that he must go to Jerusalem and suffer greatly... *Is 44:6,8, Mt 16:21*

Hail Mary...

[D]o not be afraid of those who kill the body but after that can do no more. I shall show you whom to fear. Be afraid of the one who after killing has the power to cast into Gehanna; yes, I tell you, be afraid of that one. *Lk 12:4-5*

Hail Mary...

The LORD is my light and my salvation; / whom do I fear? / ... of whom am I afraid? / ... One thing I ask of the LORD; / ... To gaze on the LORD's beauty. *Ps 27:1,4*

Hail Mary...

Beloved, we are God's children now; what we shall be has not yet been revealed. We do know that when it is revealed we shall be like him, for we shall see him as he is. *1Jn 3:2*

Hail Mary...

All of us, gazing with unveiled face on the glory of the Lord, are being transformed into the same image from glory to glory, as from the Lord who is the Spirit. *2Cor 3:18*

Hail Mary... Glory Be... O My Jesus...

The Fifth Luminous Mystery
The Institution of the Eucharist

And everywhere they bring sacrifice to my name, / and a pure offering; / For great is my name among the nations, / says the LORD of hosts. ... [W]ithout the shedding of blood there is no forgiveness. *Mal 1:11, Heb 9:22*

Our Father...

Cain brought an offering to the LORD from the fruit of the soil, while Abel, for his part, brought one of the best firstlings of his flock. ... By faith Abel offered to God a sacrifice greater than Cain's. *Gen 4:3-4, Heb 11:4*

Hail Mary...

Melchizedek, king of Salem, brought out bread and wine, and being a priest of God Most High, he blessed Abram. ... [Moses] took the blood and sprinkled it on the people, saying, "This is the blood of the covenant which the LORD has made with you." *Gen 14:18, Ex 24:8*

Hail Mary...

Clothe Aaron with the sacred vestments and anoint him, thus consecrating him as my priest ... a perpetual priesthood throughout all future generations. ... Aaron's sons, the priests ... shall then burn the whole offering on the altar as a holocaust, a sweet-smelling oblation to the LORD. *Ex 40:13,15, Lev 1:5,9*

Hail Mary...

At the time for offering sacrifice, the prophet Elijah came forward and said, "LORD, God of Abraham, Isaac ... you are God in Israel and that I am your servant." ... The LORD's fire came down and consumed the holocaust... *1Kgs 18:36,38*

Hail Mary...

THE LAST SUPPER

"[M]y Father gives you the true bread from heaven. For the bread of God is that which comes down from heaven and gives life to the world." ... "Whoever eats this bread will live forever." *Jn 6:32-33, Jn 6:58*

Hail Mary...

Then he took the bread, said the blessing, broke it, and gave it to them, saying, "This is my body, which will be given for you. ... This cup is the new covenant in my blood, which will be shed for you." *Lk 22:19-20*

Hail Mary...

"God himself will provide the sheep for the holocaust." ... Abraham built an altar there and arranged the wood on it. Next he tied up his son ... [H]e entered once for all into the sanctuary, not with the blood of goats and calves but with his own blood, thus obtaining eternal redemption. ... Golgotha. There they crucified [Jesus]. *Gen 22:8-9, Heb 9:12, Jn 19:17-18*

Hail Mary...

"Do this in remembrance of me." ... For as often as you eat the bread and drink the cup, you proclaim the death of the Lord until he comes. *1Cor 11:24,26*

Hail Mary...

"Give us each day our daily bread." ... The cup of blessing that we bless ... The bread that we break, is it not a participation in the body of Christ? Because the loaf of bread is one, we though many, are one body. *Lk 11:3, 1Cor 10:16-17*

Hail Mary...

"Like Melchizedek you are a priest forever." ... For our paschal lamb, Christ, has been sacrificed. Therefore, let us celebrate the feast ... with the unleavened bread of sincerity and truth. *Ps 110:4, 1Cor 5:7-8*

Hail Mary... Glory Be... O My Jesus... Hail Holy Queen

JESUS PRAYING IN THE GARDEN

The Sorrowful Mysteries

The Sign of the Cross

The Apostles' Creed

The end of joy may be sorrow ... My life is worn out by sorrow, / my years by sighing. / My strength fails in affliction. *Prv 14:13, Ps 31:11*

Our Father...

God is faithful and will not let you be tried beyond your strength; but with the trial he will also provide a way out, so that you may be able to bear it. *1Cor 10:13*

Hail Mary...

Most admirable and worthy of everlasting remembrance was the mother, who saw her seven sons perish in a single day, yet bore it courageously because of her hope in the Lord. *2Mc 7:20*

Hail Mary...

[Love] bears all things, believes all things, hopes all things, endures all things ... No one has greater love than this, to lay down one's life for one's friends. *1Cor 13:7, Jn 15:13*

Hail Mary... Glory be... O My Jesus...

THE AGONY IN THE GARDEN

The First Sorrowful Mystery
The Agony in the Garden

"Didn't I see you in the garden with him?" Again Peter denied it … My friends it is who wrong me; / before God my eyes drop tears. *Jn 18:26-27, Job 16:20*

Our Father…

Jesus went out with his disciples across the Kidron valley to where there was a garden. … Judas his betrayer also knew the place. *Jn 18:1-2*

Hail Mary…

Put an end to my affliction and suffering; / take away all my sins. / See how many are my enemies, / see how fiercely they hate me. *Ps 25:18-19*

Hail Mary…

When he returned to his disciples he found them asleep. He said to Peter, "So you could not keep watch with me for one hour?" *Mt 26:40*

Hail Mary…

Awake, awake! / Put on your strength, O Zion. *Is 52:1*

Hail Mary…

To strengthen him an angel from heaven appeared to him. He was in such agony and he prayed so fervently that his sweat became like drops of blood falling on the ground. *Lk 22:43-44*

Hail Mary…

ST. PETER DENYING CHRIST

I weep in bitter pain; / in accord with your word strengthen me ...
When I cried out, you answered; / you strengthened my spirit.
Ps 119:28, Ps 138:3

Hail Mary...

[Judas] went over to Jesus and said, "Hail, Rabbi!" and he kissed
him ... They laid hands on Jesus and arrested him. *Mt 26:49-50*

Hail Mary...

"Didn't I see you in the garden with him?" Again Peter denied it.
And immediately the cock crowed. *Jn 18:26-27*

Hail Mary...

"At this I weep, / my eyes run with tears: / Far from me are all who
console me, / any who might revive me; / My sons were reduced
to silence / when the enemy prevailed." *Lam 1:16*

Hail Mary...

"Simon, Simon, behold Satan has demanded to sift all of you like
wheat, but I have prayed that your own faith may not fail; and
once you have turned back, you must strengthen your brothers."
Lk 22:31-32

Hail Mary... Glory be... O My Jesus...

The Second Sorrowful Mystery
The Scourging at the Pillar

Pilate took Jesus and had him scourged ... If we are afflicted, it is for your encouragement, ... which enables you to endure the same sufferings that we suffer. *Jn 19:1, 2Cor 1:6*

Our Father...

My life is worn out by sorrow, / my years by sighing. / My strength fails in affliction; / my bones are consumed. / ... I hear the whispers of the crowd; / terrors are all around me. / They conspire against me; / they plot to take my life. *Ps 31:11,14*

Hail Mary...

"Your own nation and the chief priests handed you over to me. What have you done?" *Jn 18:35*

Hail Mary...

The chief priests and the scribes ... will mock him, spit upon him, scourge him ... Pilate took Jesus and had him scourged. *Mk 10:33-34, Jn 19:1*

Hail Mary...

What strength have I that I should endure, / and what is my limit that I should be patient? / Have I the strength of stones, / or is my flesh of bronze? *Job 6:11-12*

Hail Mary...

JESUS SCOURGED

I am mortally afflicted ... / I suffer your terrible blows. / ... your terrors have reduced me to silence. / ... my only friend is darkness. *Ps 88:16-17,19*

Hail Mary...

"O faithless and perverse generation, how long will I be with you and endure you?" *Lk 9:41*

Hail Mary...

I will make you toward this people a solid wall of brass. / Though they fight against you, / they shall not prevail, / For I am with you, / to deliver and rescue you. *Jer 15:20*

Hail Mary...

I urge you therefore, brothers, by the mercies of God, to offer your bodies as a living sacrifice, holy and pleasing to God, your spiritual worship. *Rom 12:1*

Hail Mary...

For as Christ's sufferings overflow to us, so through Christ does our encouragement also overflow. *2Cor 1:5*

Hail Mary...

Our hope for you is firm, for we know that as you share in the sufferings, you also share in the encouragement. *2Cor 1:7*

Hail Mary... Glory be... O My Jesus...

CHRIST PRESENTED TO THE PEOPLE

THE CROWN OF THORNS

The Third Sorrowful Mystery
The Crowning of Thorns

They spat upon him and took the reed and kept striking him on the head ... Our flesh had no rest, but we were afflicted in every way – external conflicts, internal fears. But God, who encourages the downcast, encouraged us. *Mt 27:30, 2Cor 7:5-6*

Our Father...

I gave my back to those who beat me, / my cheeks to those who plucked my beard; / My face I did not shield from buffets and spitting. *Is 50:6*

Hail Mary...

They spat upon him and took the reed and kept striking him on the head ... They all condemned him as deserving to die. Some began to spit on him. *Mt 27:30, Mk 14:64-65*

Hail Mary...

They spat in his face and struck him, while some slapped him ... If you are patient when you suffer for doing what is good, this is a grace before God. *Mt 26:67, 1Pt 2:20*

Hail Mary...

Yet now they sing of me in mockery. / ... They abhor me, they stand aloof from me, / they do not hesitate to spit in my face! *Job 30:9-10*

Hail Mary...

CHRIST MOCKED

They began to salute him with, "Hail, King of the Jews!" and kept striking his head with a reed and spitting upon him. *Mk 15:18-19*

Hail Mary...

All the day I am an object of laughter; everyone mocks me. *Jer 20:7*

Hail Mary...

Herod and his soldiers treated him contemptuously and mocked him ... The soldiers jeered at him. *Lk 23:11,36*

Hail Mary...

When he was insulted, he returned no insult; when he suffered, he did not threaten; instead, he handed himself over to the one who judges justly ... By his wounds you have been healed. *1Pt 2:23-24*

Hail Mary...

When persecuted, we endure; when slandered, we respond gently. We have become like the world's rubbish, the scum of all, to this very moment. *1Cor 4:12-13*

Hail Mary...

Blessed are you when they insult you and persecute you and utter every kind of evil against you [falsely] because of me ... In the last time there will live scoffers who will live according to their own godless desires. *Mt 5:11, Jude 18*

Hail Mary...Glory Be...O My Jesus...

The Fourth Sorrowful Mystery
The Carrying of the Cross

They took Jesus, and carrying the cross himself he went out to what is called the Place of the Skull ... We are always courageous ... for we walk by faith, not by sight. *Jn 19:16-17, 2Cor 5:6-7*

Our Father...

"We were utterly weighed down beyond our strength, so that we despaired even of life. Indeed, we had accepted within ourselves the sentence of death, that we might trust not in ourselves but in God who raises the dead." *2Cor 1:8-9*

Hail Mary...

Whoever does not carry his own cross and come after me cannot be my disciple. *Lk 14:27*

Hail Mary...

It was our infirmities that he bore, / our sufferings that he endured ... [laying] upon him the guilt of us all. *Is 53:4*

Hail Mary...

They took hold of a certain Simon, a Cyrenian, ... and after laying the cross on him, they made him carry it behind Jesus. ... What help you give to the powerless, what strength to the feeble arm! *Lk 23:26, Job 26:2*

Hail Mary...

JESUS FALLING BENEATH THE CROSS

NAILING CHRIST TO THE CROSS

I will also take some of the spirit that is on you and will bestow it on them, that they may share the burden of the people with you. You will then not have to bear it by yourself. *Num 11:17*

Hail Mary...

Strengthen the hands that are feeble, / make firm the knees that are weak. / ... Be strong, fear not!... We are not discouraged; rather, although our outer self is wasting away, our inner self is being renewed day by day. *Is 35:3-4, 2Cor 4:16*

Hail Mary...

"My yoke is easy, and my burden light" ... Bear one another's burdens, and so you will fulfill the law of Christ. *Mt 11:30, Gal 6:2*

Hail Mary...

Let us rid ourselves of every burden and sin that clings to us and persevere in running the race that lies before us while keeping our eyes fixed on Jesus... *Heb 12:11-12*

Hail Mary...

For to this you have been called, because Christ also suffered for you, leaving you an example that you should follow in his footsteps. / "He committed no sin." *1Pt 2:21-2*

Hail Mary...

For this momentary light affliction is producing for us an eternal weight of glory beyond all comparison, as we look not to what is seen but to what is unseen ... what is unseen is eternal. *2Cor 4:17-18*

Hail Mary... Glory be... O My Jesus...

The Fifth Sorrowful Mystery
The Crucifixion

For Christ, while we were still helpless, yet died at the appointed time for the ungodly. Indeed, only with difficulty does one die for a just person, though perhaps for a good person one might even find courage to die. *Rom 5:6-7*

Our Father...

For the sake of the joy that lay before him he endured the cross. *Heb 12:2*

Hail Mary...

Standing by the cross of Jesus were his mother ... Mary of Magdala ... and the disciple there whom he loved. *Jn 19:25*

Hail Mary...

Pilate also had an inscription written and put on the cross. It read, "Jesus the Nazorean, the King of the Jews." *Jn 19:19*

Hail Mary...

He surrendered himself to death / and was counted among the wicked ... With him they crucified two revolutionaries, one on his right and one on his left. *Is 53:12, Mk 15:27*

Hail Mary...

THE CRUCIFIXION

"Let him come down from the cross now, and we will believe in him." *Mt 27:42*

Hail Mary...

He emptied himself / taking the form of a slave ... / becoming obedient to death, / even death on a cross. *Phil 2:7-8*

Hail Mary...

"Whoever does not take up his cross and follow after me is not worthy of me." *Mt 10:38*

Hail Mary...

[Jesus] said this signifying by what kind of death [Peter] would glorify God. And when he had said this, he said to him, "Follow me." *Jn 21:19*

Hail Mary...

"If anyone wishes to come after me, he must deny himself and take up his cross daily and follow me." *Lk 9:23*

Hail Mary...

The message of the cross is foolishness to those who are perishing, but to us who are being saved it is the power of God ... Blest is the wood through which justice comes about. *1Cor 1:18, Wis 14:7*

Hail Mary... Glory be... O My Jesus...
Hail Holy Queen...

THE DESCENT FROM THE CROSS

THE BURIAL OF CHRIST

The Glorious Mysteries

The Sign of the Cross

The Apostles' Creed

I am afflicted and in pain; / let your saving help protect me, God, / That I may praise God's name in song / and glorify it with thanksgiving. *Ps 69:30-31*

Our Father...

I long to see you, that I may share with you some spiritual gift so that you may be strengthened, that is, that you and I may be mutually encouraged by one another's faith. *Rom 1:11-12*

Hail Mary...

If we hope for what we do not see, we wait with endurance ... For this we toil and struggle, because we have set our hope on the living God. *Rom 8:25, 1Tm 4:10*

Hail Mary...

May the God of endurance and encouragement grant you to think in harmony with one another, in keeping with Christ Jesus, that with one accord you may with one voice glorify the God and Father of our Lord Jesus Christ. *Rom 15:5-6*

Hail Mary... Glory be... O My Jesus...

The First Glorious Mystery
The Resurrection

From noon onward, darkness came over the whole land until three in the afternoon ... You plunged me into the bottom of the pit, / into the darkness of the abyss. *Mt 27:45, Ps 88:7*

Our Father...

Woe to those who call evil good and good evil, / who change darkness into light, and light into darkness... *Is 5:20*

Hail Mary...

Let all who dwell in the land tremble, / for the day of the LORD is coming; / Yes, it is near, a day of darkness and of gloom, / a day of clouds and somberness! *Jl 2:1-2*

Hail Mary...

Rejoice not over me, O my enemy! / though I have fallen, I will arise; / though I sit in darkness, the LORD is my light. *Mi 7:8*

Hail Mary...

The darkness is passing away, and the true light is already shining ... The earth was a formless wasteland, and darkness covered the abyss ... Then God said, "Let there be light," and there was light. *1Jn 2:8, Gen 1:2-3*

Hail Mary...

THE RESURRECTION

You alone can raise me from the gates of death. / Then I will declare all your praises, / sing joyously of your salvation / in the gates of daughter Zion. *Ps 9:14-15*

Hail Mary...

But at daybreak on the first day of the week they took the spices they had prepared and went to the tomb. ... I will sing of your strength, / extol your love at dawn. *Lk 24:1, Ps 59:17*

Hail Mary...

Where are your plagues, O death! / where is your sting, O nether world ... "Death is swallowed up in victory." *Hos 13:14, 1Cor 15:54*

Hail Mary...

For you were once darkness, but now you are light in the Lord. Live as children of light, for light produces every kind of goodness and righteousness and truth. *Eph 5:8-9*

Hail Mary...

Let us then throw off the works of darkness [and] put on the armor of light. *Rom 13:12*

Hail Mary...

God is light, and in him there is no darkness at all ... If we walk in the light as he is in the light, then we have fellowship with one another, and the blood of his Son Jesus Christ cleanses us from all sin. *1Jn 1:5,7*

Hail Mary... Glory be... O My Jesus...

The Second Glorious Mystery
The Ascension

"I came from the Father and have come into the world. Now I am leaving the world and going back to the Father ... I have told you this so that you might have peace in me. In the world you will have trouble, but take courage." *Jn 16:28,33*

Our Father...

When Jesus finished these words, he left Galilee and went to the district of Judea across the Jordan ... After he placed his hands on them, he went away. *Mt 19:1,15*

Hail Mary...

When Jesus finished these parables, he went away from there ... [Jesus] withdrew in a boat to a deserted place by himself. *Mt 13:53, Mt 14:13*

Hail Mary...

Jesus went from that place and withdrew to the region of Tyre and Sidon ... When he had taken leave of them, he went off to the mountain to pray. *Mt 15:21, Mk 6:46*

Hail Mary...

At daybreak, Jesus left and went to a deserted place. The crowds went looking for him, and when they came to him, they tried to prevent him from leaving them. *Lk 4:42*

Hail Mary...

THE ASCENSION

Since Jesus knew that they were going to come and carry him off to make him king, he withdrew again to the mountain alone. *Jn 6:15*

Hail Mary...

After he had said this, Jesus left and hid from them. Although he had performed so many signs in their presence they did not believe in him. *Jn 12:36-37*

Hail Mary...

An evil and unfaithful generation seeks a sign, but no sign will be given it except the sign of Jonah. Then he left them and went away. *Mt 16:4*

Hail Mary...

Jesus said to [Mary], "Stop holding on to me, for I have not yet ascended to the Father. But go to my brothers and tell them, 'I am going to my Father and your Father, to my God and your God.' " *Jn 20:17*

Hail Mary...

I will be with you as I was with Moses: I will not leave you nor forsake you ... "I will never forsake you or abandon you." *Jos 1:5, Heb 13:5*

Hail Mary...

As he blessed them he parted from them and was taken up to heaven ... [taking] his seat at the right of the throne of God. *Lk 24:51, Heb 12:2*

Hail Mary... Glory be... O My Jesus...

The Third Glorious Mystery
The Descent of the Holy Spirit

They were all filled with the holy Spirit ... After we had suffered, ... we drew courage through our God to speak to you the gospel of God with much struggle. *Acts 2:4, 1Thes 2:2*

Our Father...

"Go therefore, and make disciples of all nations, baptizing them in the name of the Father, and of the Son, and of the holy Spirit." *Mt 28:19*

Hail Mary...

They will seize and persecute you, they will hand you over to the synagogues and to prisons, and they will have you led before kings and governors because of my name. *Lk 21:12*

Hail Mary...

On that day, there broke out a severe persecution of the church in Jerusalem. *Acts 8:1*

Hail Mary...

In zeal I persecuted the church ... "Saul, Saul, why are you per-secuting me" ... "I am Jesus, whom you are persecuting." *Phil 3:6, Acts 9:4-5*

Hail Mary...

THE DESCENT OF THE SPIRIT

They only kept hearing that "the one who was persecuting us is now preaching the faith he once tried to destroy." So they glorified God because of me. *Gal 1:23-24*

Hail Mary...

"For I am the least of the apostles, not fit to be called an apostle, because I persecuted the Church of God. But by the grace of God I am what I am." *1Cor 15:9-10*

Hail Mary...

"What will separate us from the love of Christ? Will anguish, or distress, or persecution...?" *Rom 8:35*

Hail Mary...

Put up with hardship; perform the work of an evangelist; fulfill your ministry ... All who want to live religiously in Christ will be persecuted. *2Tm 4:5, 2Tm 3:12*

Hail Mary...

You have followed my teaching, way of life, purpose, faith, patience, love, endurance, persecutions, and sufferings ... Encourage through all patience and teaching. *2Tm 3:10, 2Tm 4:2*

Hail Mary...

Blessed are they who are persecuted for the sake of righteousness, / for theirs is the kingdom of heaven. *Mt 5:10*

Hail Mary... Glory be... O My Jesus...

The Fourth Glorious Mystery
The Assumption of the Blessed Virgin Mary into Heaven

If we have died with him / we shall live with him; / if we persevere / we shall also reign with him ... Yet we are courageous, and we would rather leave the body and go home to the Lord. *2Tm 2:11-12, 2Cor 5:8*

Our Father...

The one who peers into the perfect law of freedom and perseveres, and is not a hearer who forgets but a doer who acts, such a one shall be blessed in what he does. *Jas 1:25*

Hail Mary...

"So mighty is God, / our God who leads us always!" *Ps 48:15*

Hail Mary...

I am made glorious in the sight of the LORD, / and my God is now my strength! *Is 49:5*

Hail Mary...

We call blessed those who have persevered. *Jas 5:11*

Hail Mary...

You alone can raise me from the gates of death. / Then I will declare all your praises, / sing joyously of your salvation. *Ps 9:14-15*

Hail Mary...

He who fears the LORD will have a happy end; / even on the day of his death he will be blessed ... "Behold, from now on will all ages call me blessed." *Sir 1:11, Lk 1:48*

Hail Mary...

Remain faithful until death, and I will give you the crown of life. *Rv 2:10*

Hail Mary...

We know that we have passed from death to life because we love our brothers. *1Jn 3:14*

Hail Mary...

"He will wipe every tear from their eyes, and there shall be no more death or mourning, wailing or pain, [for] the old order has passed away." *Rv 21:4*

Hail Mary...

For whatever was written previously was written for our instruction, that by endurance and by the encouragement of the scriptures we might have hope ... The one who perseveres to the end will be saved. *Rom 15:5, Mt 24:13*

Hail Mary... Glory be... O My Jesus...

The Fifth Glorious Mystery
The Coronation of the Blessed Virgin Mary, Queen of Heaven and Earth

God's temple in heaven was opened, and the ark of his covenant could be seen in the temple ... A woman clothed with the sun ... was with child and wailed aloud in pain... *Rv 11:19, Rv 12:1-2*

Our Father...

Cease your cries of mourning, / wipe the tears from your eyes. / The sorrow you have shown shall have its reward. *Jer 31:16*

Hail Mary...

If, then, we have died with Christ, we believe that we shall also live with him ... I consider that the sufferings of this present time are as nothing compared with the glory to be revealed for us. *Rom 6:8, Rom 8:18*

Hail Mary...

Even if you should suffer because of righteousness, blessed are you ... "Behold, from now on will all ages call me blessed." *1Pt 3:14, Lk 1:48*

Hail Mary...

If [one] part suffers, all the parts suffer with it; if one part is honored, all the parts share its joy. *1Cor 12:26*

Hail Mary...

THE CROWNED VIRGIN: A VISION OF JOHN

For whenever anyone bears the pain of unjust suffering because of consciousness of God, that is a grace … "Hail, [Mary]! The Lord is with you." *1Pt 2:19, Lk 1:28*

Hail Mary...

For to this you have been called, because Christ also suffered for you, leaving you an example that you should follow in his footsteps. *1Pt 2:21*

Hail Mary...

The God of all grace who called you to his eternal glory through Christ [Jesus] will himself restore, confirm, strengthen, and establish you after you have suffered a little. *1Pt 5:10*

Hail Mary...

For the Son of Man will come with his angels in his Father's glory, and then he will repay everyone according to his conduct. *Mt 16:27*

Hail Mary...

Rejoice to the extent that you share in the sufferings of Christ, so that when his glory is revealed you may also rejoice exultantly. *1Pt 4:13*

Hail Mary...

"Behold, I am coming soon. I bring with me the recompense I will give to each according to his deeds. I am the Alpha and the Omega." *Rv 22:12*

Hail Mary... Glory be... O My Jesus...
Hail Holy Queen...

The Prayers of the Most Holy Rosary

The Apostles' Creed

I believe in God, the Father Almighty, Creator of heaven and earth; and in Jesus Christ, His only Son, our Lord; who was conceived by the Holy Spirit, born of the Virgin Mary, suffered under Pontius Pilate, was crucified, died, and was buried. He descended into Hell; the third day He arose again from the dead; He ascended into Heaven, sitteth at the right hand of God, the Father Almighty; from thence He shall come to judge the living and the dead. I believe in the Holy Spirit, the Holy Catholic Church, the Communion of Saints, the forgiveness of sins, the resurrection of the body, and life everlasting. Amen.

Our Father

Our Father, Who art in Heaven, hallowed be Thy Name. Thy kingdom come; Thy will be done on earth as it is in Heaven. Give us this day our daily bread, and forgive us our trespasses, as we forgive those who trespass against us. And lead us not into temptation, but deliver us from evil. Amen.

Hail Mary

Hail Mary, full of grace, the Lord is with thee; blessed art thou among women, and blessed is the Fruit of thy womb, Jesus. Holy Mary, Mother of God, pray for us sinners, now and at the hour of our death. Amen.

Glory Be

Glory be to the Father, and to the Son, and to the Holy Spirit. As it was in the beginning, is now, and ever shall be, world without end. Amen.

O My Jesus

O My Jesus, forgive us our sins; save us from the fires of Hell, lead all souls to Heaven, especially those who are in most need of Thy Mercy.

Hail, Holy Queen

Hail, holy Queen, Mother of mercy, our life, our sweetness and our hope. To thee do we cry, poor banished children of Eve! To thee do we send up our sighs, mourning and weeping in this valley of tears. Turn then, most gracious advocate, thine eyes of mercy towards us. And after this, our exile, show unto us the blessed Fruit of thy womb, Jesus. O clement, O loving, O sweet Virgin Mary.

Pray for us, O holy Mother of God, that we may be made worthy of the promises of Christ.

Prayer after the Rosary

O God, whose only begotten Son, by His life, death and resurrection, has purchased for us the rewards of eternal life; grant, we beseech Thee, that, meditating upon these mysteries of the Most Holy Rosary of the Blessed Virgin Mary, we may imitate what they contain and obtain what they promise, through the same Christ our Lord. Amen.

May the divine assistance remain always with us. And may the souls of the faithful departed, through the mercy of God, rest in peace. Amen.

Other Works by Christine Haapala

His Sorrowful Passion is a prayer book that integrates Sacred Scripture meditations with the prayers of the Chaplet of Divine Mercy. This prayer book includes two Scriptural Chaplets of Divine Mercy: one chronicles Jesus' Passion and the other features the Seven Penitential Psalms. The woodcuts of the 15th century Catholic artist, Albrecht Dürer, illustrate this book. Time for Mercy is a CD Recording of the Seven Penitential Psalms Chaplet of Divine Mercy from His Sorrowful Passion. Singer and composer Nancy Scimone's new chaplet melody is featured with meditations led by Brother Leonard Konopka, MIC. Additionally, an instrumental version of the Chaplet of Divine Mercy is included on the Time for Mercy CD.

Speak, Lord, I am Listening is a prayer book that presents the richness of the Sacred Mysteries of the Most Holy Rosary allowing children to visualize and to understand. Gus Muller's watercolors express the depths of the agony of Christ crucified and reach the heights of the Blessed Virgin Mary's glorious reign as Queen of Heaven and Earth. Succinct and apt meditation selections yield a wealth of spiritual insight into the mysterious events of the lives of Jesus and Mary.

The Sanctity of Life Scriptural Rosary is a recorded prayer with over 150 Sacred Scripture verses revealing God's message of the dignity and sanctity of life intertwined with the prayers of the Most Holy Rosary and accompanied by Nancy Scimone's original meditative piano music.

From Genesis to Revelation: Seven Scriptural Rosaries called "the encyclopedia of Scriptural Rosaries" is the most extensive collection of Scriptural Rosaries you will find in one book. Each of the seven Scriptural Rosaries contains a thematic set of Sacred Scripture quotations that are specially selected to accompany and illuminate meditation on the mysteries of the Rosary from the books of the Old and New Testament. Pray the Rosary with Jesus and

Mary, pray the Rosary with Sts. Peter and Paul, pray the Rosary with the Old Testament prophets, and many more.

Ordering Information

To purchase additional copies of this book or the other works mentioned above, please visit your local Catholic bookstore or visit us on-line at www.sufferingservant.com. Individual orders or quantity discounts are also available by calling Suffering Servant Scriptorium at 1-888-652-9494.